@AnnalisaTricori
Tricori Series/ Journal
https://annalisatricori.com

THIS JOURNAL BELONGS TO:

- -

www.ingramcontent.com/pod-product-compliance
Lightning Source LLC
Chambersburg PA
CBHW080932170526
45158CB00008B/2258